Quiet Eyes

Glenda J. Eddings

Quiet Eyes
Copyright © 2025 by Glenda J. Eddings

ISBN: 979-8894792194 (sc)
ISBN: 979-8894792200 (e)

The Reading Glass Books
1-888-420-3050
www.readingglassbooks.com
production@readingglassbooks.com

Quiet Eyes

Quiet Eyes

When we look with quiet eyes

we see another's heart

we can place our hand upon our own

we know we are connected

When we look with quiet eyes

we can sense another's joy

a thousand griefs can disappear

when we ourselves smile.

When we look with quiet eyes

We can sense another's pain

when first we become friends

with our own and accept it.

When we look with quiet eyes

we can understand another

reaching out in faith

offering our own experience.

The Next Time You Wonder

The next time you wonder

Why am I here?

Think of those who are no longer with us.

The next time you wonder

Of what significance am I?

Remember the time you once helped a friend.

The next time you wonder

Is loving worth something?

Think of hate which is nothing.

The next time you wonder

Why have my eyes seen so much pain?

Think of those who are blind, who have

seen only darkness.

The next time you wonder

Why all the lies?

Seek to find the truth, and when found

become one with it.

Fantasy Circus

I want to be a clown

Through laughing eyes I would peer

And see life on its funny side

Never having to shed a tear.

I want to be a clown

So I would laugh at me

And then I would paint the world

In beautiful colors everyone could see.

I want to be a clown

Everyone knows they never cry

And clowns always say hello

They never say goodbye.

I want to be a clown

I would never feel pain or strife

And each day would be a circus

But I would never understand life,

Maybe instead of being a clown

For all the world to see

I will leave the circus just for now

And try starting to be me.

A Child's Heart

A child's heart is fragile

yet we hold it in our hand every day

A child's smile is a birth right

yet we often wipe tears away

A child's mind is learning

yet we are called to put teaching there

A child's ears are keen

yet God's word they are called to hear

How often should we ask ourselves,

"Dear God, thy will be done,"

When we are called upon to care

for these precious little ones

What an honor and a privilege

this calling we impart

being called by our heavenly father

to teach a child's heart

He's Two

He's two

and he does such strange things

like looking at the world upside

down.

He's two

and he does such strange things

like seeing things in color and never

black and white.

He's two

but only in human years

a beautiful mind, a beautiful heart

He has taught me TO accept all things

He's two

and he does such strange things

living in his own little world

I want TO live there TOO.

Snow Falling On Tears (For Gabriel)

He was so young

Taken by a thief in the night

Called mortality

Standing in silence

Snow falling on tears

I breathe deeply

and silently cry

for a little boy

who will never become a man.

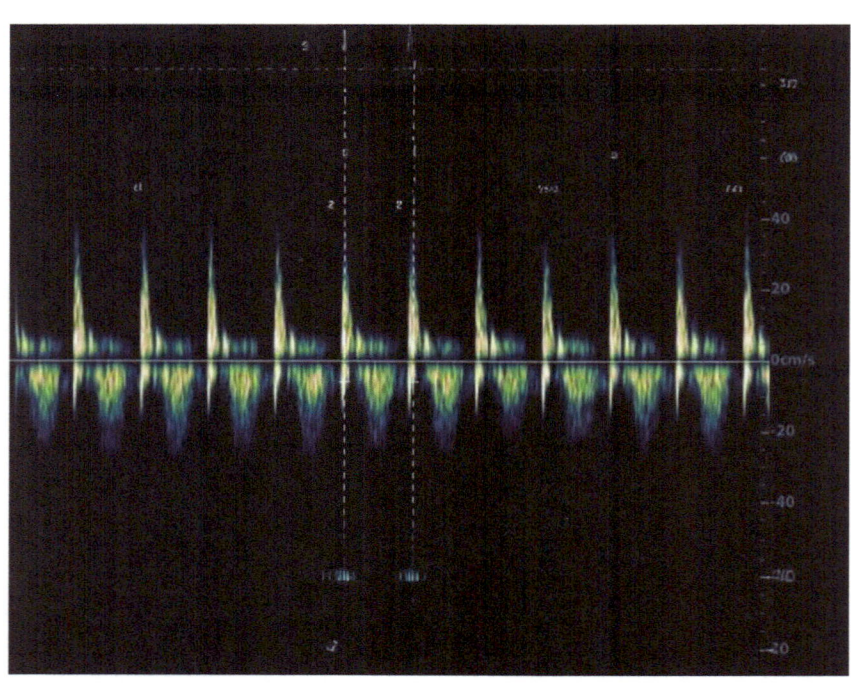

Dancing Under My Heart

I felt a strange sensation

A feeling I could not impart

A pair of delicate angel wings

Dancing under my heart.

First they were rather subtle

I could barely feel them there

Then I began to wonder

If someone was living there.

I remembered all beautiful rainbows seen

But had never given a thought

To the beauty of such a miracle

That was dancing under my heart.

Through Her Eyes

Golden locks of hair

Sparkling eyes of green

When baby sleeps

What is her dream?

Her years are so few

Yet there is wisdom there

She represents the best in us

Her trusting casts out fear

Beautiful tiny girl

Wrapped in innocent bliss

Wake up the world

With your fairy kiss.

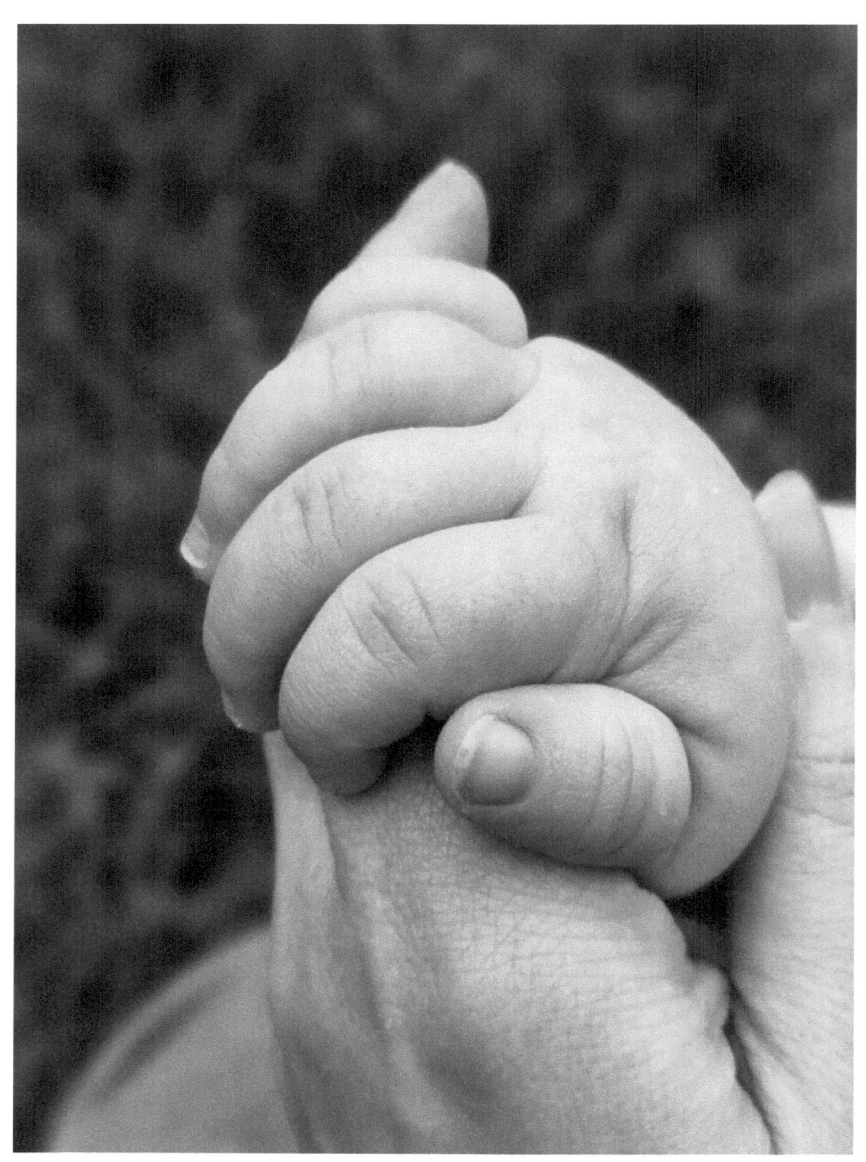

Embryo of a God

The small seed

Planted by love

Nourished by the Deity's hand

Began to move-It was alive.

The womb lay waiting

Strength of a mother's love

Had been prepared for giving.

The small seed

Was bigger now

Encasing the potential

Of all miracles.

The embryo was finally grown

A world waited to welcome

This new spiritual prophet

With the thrust of great anxiety

A new god was born

He had left his principalities

To enter our world with a cry.

Reemergence

When I was a child

I used to blow bubbles.

I enjoyed chasing rainbows

The world seemed free from troubles.

When I was a child

I used to count stars

I loved my stuffed toys

The world seemed free from wars.

When I was a child

I used to paint skies

I adored my best friend

The world seemed free from lies.

As I began to grow

My bubbles turned to plastic illusions

My rainbows turned to gray

The world to confusion.

As I began to grow

The stars became harder to find

my toys turned to expensive motor cars

Conflict found a home in my mind.

As I began to grow

My skies became filled with pollution

My friends to mere acquaintances

In my heart there seemed no solution.

So much for childish dreams and aspirations

They die so quickly as adulthood wishes.

Open the Cage

Open the cage

Your life awaits

Your spirit is free

Among the chaos

which has held you captive.

Hurtful words, suspicious stares

Others who dismiss you, let it go.

Open the cage

You are not merely a bird

With wings clipped and fragile

But rather a free spirit.

A heart, a mind, a soul

To be reckoned with.

You are free, own it!

Fly high!

Even beyond yourself.

Angel Wings

Today a life ended

And another one was born

One received by the Savior

Another just left his arms.

In our trials and tribulations

It's often hard to see

The beauty of our life on Earth

And someday Heavens Majesty.

Though we shall cry while we are here

There also will be laughter

God calls us to enjoy this life

Before we leave for our life hereafter

So when your heart seems heavy

And you doubt what another day brings

Remember you are always held up

By the strength of Angel Wings.

Awareness

Be not ashamed you cried in my presence, friend.

Because of the experience I love you more.

I saw not the tears streaming down your face

But rather a heart which said,

I feel.

Flight 911
Dedicated To our Troops

I see sorrow on their faces

I see sadness in their eyes

I told them I was leavin'

It should have come as no surprise.

I wish that I could hold them

And tell them how I feel

Before this plane leaves from the ground

And the people become unreal.

I hear the engines beginning

As the tears fill my eyes

I told them I was leavin'

It should have come as no surprise.

Unsung Hero

I want to be a hero said the little boy

As he grasped the plastic gun-his favorite toy

I wanna grow up to be big and tall

So I can build fences and concrete walls.

N HELTON

OLBERT SA\

EDDINGS

N JARMON

S LINDER E.

RGER SCRUG

RRESON

Legacy

I am part of something greater than myself

All those before me

Have left footsteps for me to follow.

I am to choose, however, my own path.

To imitate my ancestors

or those who came before

Would eliminate my own gifts to humanity.

To raise my children in truth and righteousness

This will be my legacy.

Photo taken at the Legacy

Museum in Montgomery, Alabama

Small Hands To Hold

He once was her husband

His countenance stood bold

He promised he would never leave the children

And their small hands to hold.

He once was her lover

His eyes spoke of song

He promised he would never leave the children

and their small hands to hold.

He once was her best friend

His heart was never cold

He promised he would never leave the children and their

small hands to hold.

She once was his wife

His love she could not hold

She promised she would always love the children

and their small hands to hold.

She once was his lover

But their life was all wrong

She promised she would always love the children

and their small hands to hold.

She once was his best friend

Now she is alone

And the children have each other

with their small hands to hold.

There's Nothing Funny About Being A Purple Pony

Purple ponies are rejected by their mothers

Hated by their fathers and ridiculed by others.

Purple ponies are made to feel small

Other colts don't care how they feel at all.

They are running in a different horse race.

Purple ponies in numbers are few indeed

But they never fit in with society.

Purple ponies are a unique kind of breed

In between the lines they learn to read.

Thank God for the purple ponies

The world has too many yellow phonies.

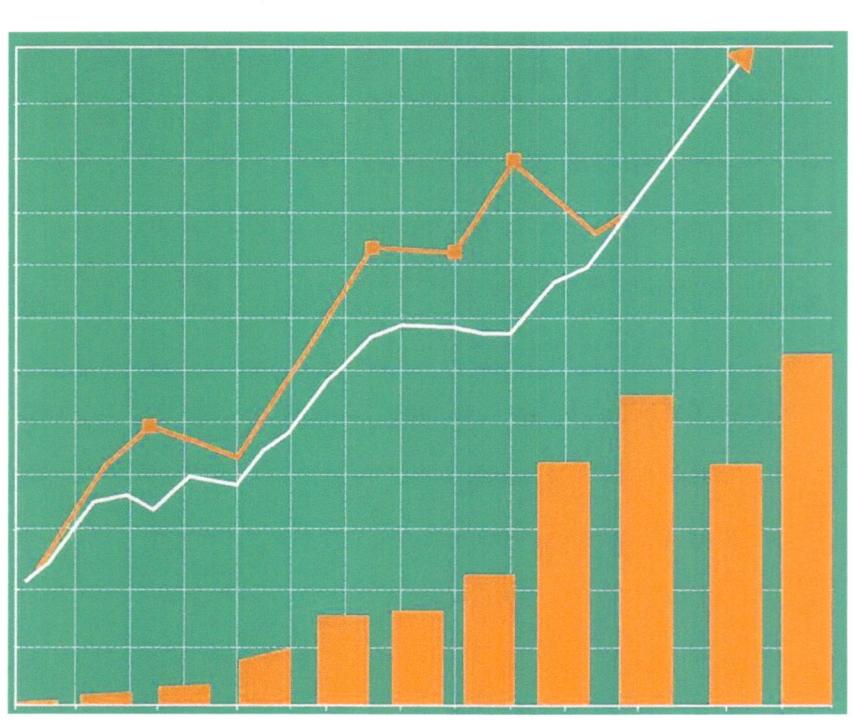

Statistics are a bore

Statistics are a bore

When they try to explain life

In terms of numbers

Statistics are a bore

When they try to explain intelligence

In terms of non-existence norms.

Statistics are a bore

When they try to explain populations

by "random guessing"

Statistics are a bore, period!

When Dandelions Smile

When Dandelions smile

The world stands still

To appreciate their beauty

On a silent hill.

When dandelions smile

The clouds depart Casting golden shadows

Upon the human heart

When dandelions smile

The world gives new birth

To all living things

Embraced by Mother Earth

He's My Savior

I follow in his footsteps,

Every day of my life,

He helps me when I fall,

From sorrow grief or strife.

He hears me and He listens,

Every time I pray,

He gives me scriptures and commandments,

And wants me to obey.

He sent me a protector,

I've had since I was eight,

He guides me to always choose the right,

When temptation is so great.

Sometimes I feel alone and lonely,

In this cold dark place,

But I know that thou art with me,

Through every trial I must face.

He told me love my enemies,

He told me love my neighbor,

He taught me compassion and kindness

And that's why He's my Savior.

- Gabriella Eddings

There are sharks in the ocean.

But there also may be Mermaids

Material things don't last

But heart ties last forever.

No matter what the odds

Run your race.

www.ingramcontent.com/pod-product-compliance
Lightning Source LLC
Chambersburg PA
CBHW040849120626

46547CB00001B/88